LEARNING THRU DISCUSSION

by Wm. FAWCETT HILL

with an Introduction by HERBERT A. THELEN

SAGE PUBLICATIONS / BEVERLY HILLS LONDON

For information address:

SAGE PUBLICATIONS, INC.
275 South Beverly Drive
Beverly Hills, California 90212

SAGE PUBLICATIONS LTD
St George's House / 44 Hatton Garden
London EC1N 8ER

Eleventh printing, revised edition

Printed in the United States of America

International Standard Book Number 0-8039-0044-9

Library of Congress Catalog Card No. 78-87064

IN MEMORY OF

NORA J. GROSS

ACKNOWLEDGMENTS

The material presented in this manual stems from two main sources. One source is a previous pamphlet published by the Center for the Study of Liberal Education for Adults in Chicago, Notes and Essays No. 22, entitled *Learning and Teaching Thru Discussion* and authored by Ida S. Hill and Wm. Fawcett Hill. Acknowledgment is made of their permission to reprint sections from this pamphlet, in which the rationale and educational philosophy underlying the discussion-group method was dealt with quite extensively. The present publication is more of a 'How To' manual. Therefore, thoughtful instructors contemplating using this method of learning through discussion would find it helpful to consult the original presentation. The other source is with the experience gained over the past ten years with the method. LTD has been used in a variety of settings, with a wide variety of professionals and para-professionals and in teaching a variety of subject matters. The cooperation of the student nurses at Utah State Hospital and the students in introductory psychology classes at Idaho State College with LTD is gratefully acknowledged. The difficulties encountered in the execution of the method led to a sharpening of the tools and the development of techniques of reinforcement which have helped in the maximizing of the potential of the method.

Contacts over the years with our colleagues in group development have had an influence apparent on every page, but in particular the impact of Jack Gibb and Hubert Coffey is mentioned. It was Dr. Ida S. Coppolino's appreciation of Coffey's concept of group cognitive map making that led to her original formulation of the method presented here. All of the psychologists at Utah State Hospital who were on the staff from 1956 to 1961 participated in the development and utilization of the method; particularly mentioned is the supervisory work of Richard Gross and Neil Sherwood.

Finally, gratitude is expressed to the many instructors who have continued to use LTD, especially Jerome Rabow, Alan Anderson, and Don Long. The confidence of such people has encouraged me to bring out this publication.

May, 1969   Wm. Fawcett Hill
                                University of Southern California

CONTENTS

INTRODUCTION

HERBERT A. THELEN

Knowledge, we are told, can be learned for "ornamentation" or for "use"; as a possession which distinguishes middle class from lower class (let us say) or as "internalized" guidelines actually useful for intelligent, adaptive, or creative behavior. From the Depression to the present, the swing has been toward ornamentation, and the ornament most sought is the high school diploma, which separates those who will be part of the productive society from those who won't. The diploma is gotten in exchange for a passel of lesser certificates and examinations—much like getting a toaster for several books of green stamps. The certificates or test results are not actually very ornamental—I certainly would not frame one to hang in the living room; but as psychic possessions they are counted and recounted, appraised and assayed, sources of hope or despair. The chief learning route for psychic ornamentation is memorization, enumeration, quotation, and standardization. One learns to say the "right" thing in each of the situations distinguishable by members of his social community. This performance in the *role* of "student" finds its most artistic expression in test wiseness; and education is operationally definable as learning how to respond to tests by listening to lectures on the same material and by studying the lecturer who usually doubles as the test maker.

This little book is *not* about knowledge for ornamentation, learning as collecting, or how to separate the sheep from the goats. This little book is about the process of acquiring knowledge for use. It is a modest book, untroubled by pretension. It knows its place and is supremely confident and secure in that knowledge—and can therefore be really helpful to those whose expectations are realistic. Perhaps the way I can be most useful is as a middleman, trying to show just where the book fits into typical concepts of the instructional sequence and what kinds of usefulness it has. Obviously, in *Learning Thru Discussion* it is assumed that there is something to be learned, and you don't have to get very far in the book before Dr. Hill speaks of learning materials that are to be studied by the student before the discussion begins.

Generally speaking, then, educators tend to think of sequences of activities, and each sequence has a beginning and end. (The "unit" plans made this very explicit.) Thus one can think of presentation (by the teacher), recitation (catechism), and testing, as a simpleminded sort of unit—and he would be astonished to discover how well this 1870 (or earlier) sequence fits most teaching in high schools today. Or, moving up to the twenties, he might find a sequence of overview (or stimulation), presentation, assimilation, application, and evaluation. Coming to the present, he would find a number of more sophisticated inquiry models (Taba, Suchman, Thelen, et al.) which gain in precision and elegance at the expense of generality.

Any adequate conception of *instructional* sequences has to somehow make room for the student alone with the materials; the student interacting with other students; the teacher intervening to focus activity and maintain its purposive, or means-ends, function. The part of the sequence that *Learning Thru Discussion* concerns itself with is the personal-social "interactive" (person-to-person, face-to-face) use of ideas presented in learning materials.

Any adequate conception of *curriculum* has to provide a rationale for the decisions which must be made before instruction can begin. How shall we decide what purposes to realize? How shall we select or create the materials of instruction? How shall we group the students into hardworking classes? And so on. Some educators would insist that *all* of these decisions (and many more) should be made before the class assembles, as, for example, in the use of programmed learning. There are other educators who feel that *none* of these decisions should be made in advance; that students must participate in making the decisions and that such participation is necessary to "meaningful" learning. Most modern educators, particularly witting or unwitting "systems" theorists, tend to make some decisions in advance and then build into instruction the means for modifying and elaborating the decisions as one goes; that is, they would lay out the task in general terms and then rely on information gained as the work proceeds, in order to decide exactly how to intervene, how much effort to put into it, what aspirations are reasonable, how to accommodate individual differences, etc. This "systems" view underlies Hill's approach. Starting with the materials already decided upon, Hill shows the variety of ways in which the material can be pinched, punched, squeezed, kicked, and, ultimately, mastered. And he offers a plan for keeping the discussion on the beam—self-correcting, unambiguous, goal directed; one not only learns, he also knows what he has learned and what he can use it for; and it is only thus that knowledge can transfer or universalize or transcend the immediate situation in which it was learned.

One objection to any planned sequence of steps is that while it probably makes sense (perhaps) for some—such as the teacher—it cannot make sense for all. It must therefore be discriminatory. There is, of course, something to this charge of unfairness. There are certain skills one requires for any operation (including independent study), and those who have these skills have an easier time (and may learn less) than those who do not have the skills. But the implication is not that demands for skills should be thrown out, but that the situation be such that persons can get the help they need to learn the skills as they need them (which is the best time), and that they not be punished for deficiencies. The group discussion, then, should incorporate its own procedures for self-improvement, for automatic accommodation between members and group demands. A situation is, in short, unfair if one cannot meet its prerequisites of skill. It is also unfair if rewards are unavailable to some, but not to others. Thus the second implication for Learning Thru Discussion is that a wide range of rewards be available so that there is something for everybody, some realistic point in striving. The range of rewards depends on the variety of things for which one can be rewarded, and Hill's scheme is unusually powerful in its explicit recognition of the great victory of task, group, and personal "roles" which are needed and which are therefore entitled to reward. The discussion sequence, with its variety of demands from step to step, is rich—rich in stimulation and rich in reward.

The idea of any plan or program for a group to be walked through annoys some people who like to emphasize spontaneity, individuality, creativity, permissiveness, humanity, etc.; and, by the same token, the idea of a plan or program for a group may have an unholy fascination for people who like to emphasize efficiency, predictability, security, orderly "development," etc. The *necessity* for a plan is not created by either attitude. It comes from the nature of groups themselves. One would need a general method, but not a stepwise plan, if he were working by himself. If he were working with two or three others, certain phases would probably be observed to form a sequence, but the chap himself might not be at all conscious of these phases. But when the group is larger *and* when it has a common purpose (which requires people to listen to each other rather than merely to think out loud), then there has to be enough definition of expectations so that individuals know how to participate, can quite consciously guide their own behavior, and can learn from the responses it provokes in others. When two friends are chatting, they freely and easily respond to whatever the other does—changes of topic, mood, and feeling; but in a larger group, especially when the members do not know each other (that is, do not know what to expect from them), who is to say whether the topic, mood, or feeling is to be changed? And who is to say what the group should come up with, and whether the range of ideas is adequate? One obvious answer, of course, is an authoritarian leader—in which case the group spends its time studying the leader. The other answer is clarity of purpose, in which clarity is achieved both by having purposes immediately recognizable as making sense and by taking the time to rehearse quite concretely what is involved in satisfying each (as, for instance, how much time to allow). The Hill scheme substitutes methodological clarity for arbitrary leader author- ity, and it puts the leader in the role of helping the group achieve its purposes rather than in the role of making demands on the group and then (possibly hypocritically) add- ing insult to injury by offering to help the group meet these demands.

One further point in this overview: How literally or seri- ously or insistently is this formulation to be followed? Is it a line-by-line recipe to be followed in all its exquisite details? Or is it an illustration of a few guidelines whose *application* may differ markedly from one situation to the next? Or is it a set of expectations of the sort of thing productive groups do, so that no matter how the leader operates these expecta- tions will be discernible within the system? One may, I think, take it in all these ways. But I think there is a common element underlying all the ways to use the formulation: it is a *conceptual model* against which practice can be compared and (hopefully) better penetrated and understood. I would suggest that one must face up to this model; if he want to modify it, leave out steps, place them in a different sequence, change the house rules—then he must explain to himself why; the burden of proof lies on him, not on the model. The beginner, I think, should literally touch all the bases in several sequences and, in the process, "internalize" the ideas of role, cooperation, function, control, etc. Then I think he will find himself beginning to make small variations, moving back and forth with previews and reviews even while following the main track. Ultimately a person might want to explicate his own ideas of some different logic of sequence and try them out; surely some differences would be expected depending on differences in the disciplines from which the learning materials come. Ideas, even as beautifully reasoned as Hill's, must finally free, not enslave, the teacher, and the features that finally remain as requirements are just those that ensure him the greatest scope for development of *his own* precious (and needed) abilities.

Professor Thelen is at the School of Education, University of Chicago.

THE ROLE OF LEARNING IN GROUP DISCUSSION

EVER SINCE THE American Revolution the democratic way of life has been endorsed as the American way of life. Except for the electoral system, democracy as a way of life has in reality been resisted and for a very simple reason—it challenges the position of the vested authorities. There is a modern revolution which has gained great impetus in the last two decades and is characterized by the actual utilization of democratic concepts in many fields of human endeavor rather than confining them exclusively to the polling booth. It is termed a revolution because, as a social development, it is relatively rapid (although long heralded and long honored in the breach) and because it represents a partial overthrow of the traditional authority of such figures as the teacher, the therapist, the boss or owner, and the parent. The revolution has been carried out through the development of group work, which involves the recognition and utilization of the properties and potentials of the small face-to-face group. For a society to be truly democratic, it must in some way extend democratic principles to this fundamental social unit—the primary group. The evidence for asserting that such a revolution exists is partially provided by the phenomenal growth of participation in discussion groups, psychotherapy groups, conference groups, workshop groups and social group work as well as the rapid development in the science of group dynamics.

As in all revolutions, there are abuses carried on in the name of democracy, and this is certainly true in the democratizing of the classroom. The discussion group, which is the topic of this article, has been the principal influence in introducing democratic principles into the educational process, and in so doing has undoubtedly been guilty of abuses and excesses. Because of this, and also because it does challenge the authority of the teacher, it is hardly surprising that there is much criticism directed at the discussion-group approach. Much of it can be readily turned against the critics and the traditional position they apparently defend. We prefer to take the criticism seriously rather than deflect it, even though we are obviously biased toward the group approach. The reason for this stems from the fact that we are uneasy about current practices in group discussion. When the barbs are removed, and the arguments against group discussion reduced to a common denominator, the salient objection of the critics is that the discussion group seriously vitiates the contribution of the highly trained and well-informed instructor. When the barbs are reinserted, the discussion group is often referred to as a case of 'the blind leading the blind,' or as an instance of people coming together to pool their ignorance.

Analysis of studies of discussion groups indicates that the discussion-group method did not emerge as superior in terms of academic achievement, interest in the course, increased skill in subject matter and so forth. On the other hand, it was not found to be inferior. Our review of these studies did supply the clue which led us to reexamine our assumptions about discussion in the classroom. The clue lay in the words used to describe the discussion method employed in the experimental settings—words like *unstructured, permissive, uncontrolled,* and *student centered.* These words, all of which sound reminiscent of the Dewey-eyed educators of an earlier era and, like them, in a reaction to authoritarian methods, may be emphasizing the pleasure principle at the expense of the reality principle, and confounding laissez faire with democratic principles. If discussion groups are run along lines more appropriate to therapy groups, the validity of the foregoing criticism must be recognized and dealt with. Before dealing with the apparent weaknesses in the discussion-group approach, it is nonetheless remarkable that so much success has been claimed for this method by those who admittedly run groups under unstructured and often unsupervised conditions. There are in the literature many testimonials, sometimes backed up by student evaluations and by grades achieved, which contrast favorably with control groups. These testimonials claim, in addition to comparable results in terms of performance on examinations, superiority in the significant areas of student involvement and enthusiasm for learning and even in the area of personality development. The sheer weight of testimony for the discussion-group approach is almost overwhelming. There seems to be little doubt that the discussion group will usually produce more personalized emotional effects of an educationally desirable nature, and we will not dwell on this point further. Nevertheless, we are not completely overwhelmed and cannot help noticing that the majority of teaching is done by the traditional methods and in fact, many of the advocates of the discussion group desert the method any time that subject matter of any degree of difficulty must be thoroughly mastered. In short, the discussion method is usually reserved for such courses as Marriage and the Modern Family, Understanding Modern Art, or Citizenship. Even the critics agree that the discussion group is good if the goal is attitude formation or opinion-sharing. The question that is of concern in this pamphlet is whether group discussion can be used effectively to meet stringent requirements of subject matter mastery. The position taken here is that mastery of difficult material can be achieved through the discussion group, but not through permissive and unstructured approaches.

The main point that we would like to make is that in using the discussion-group approach the teacher is involved in *group work* as well as the content of the course. If the group is to be used as an educational device, which is presumably the rationale for not lecturing in the first place, then the instructor needs to have some knowledge of group process, group development, and group dynamics. Most instructors who 'have tried it and didn't like it' did not have any sophistication in group techniques; failure and frustration could have readily been anticipated. One principle of group work at issue here is that, for a group to achieve its objectives, the members need to have some understanding of the roles they must execute. The typical student in our culture has had little preparation for participation in a discussion group as his academic experience has been dominated by lecture methods. Thus the students and the group flounder and turn to the instructor for help. Due to the instructor's own lack of understanding of group work, or his allegiance to permissivity, he usually cannot or will not provide the training necessary for a productive learning group. A partial remedy for this situation would be for the leader to consult one of the many excellent discussion leader guides that are available. However, excellent as they may be, they are more concerned with how to lead a lively discussion than with accomplishing the learning task. This pamphlet was prepared to provide for this need on the part of leaders or group members. This guide is not intended to supplant, but to supplement, other guides for discussion-group leaders.

As might already have been anticipated, we advocate, where didactic material must be mastered, that the discussion group have some method of proceeding. It must have a plan, a map, a program, or some agreed-upon procedure, and the idea that any random comment is appropriate grist for the mill is firmly rejected. Something other than free association by the whole group or domination by one member is indicated. Even if a student agrees that these things are not desirable, he nonetheless does not know how to proceed, and if he has some idea, it is in all likelihood not congruent with anyone else's. Thus the group is usually paralyzed and cannot take any productive steps forward. The instructor should have and should communicate some method for the group to carry on the discussion of the assigned topic.

Our analysis of these studies of discussion groups also revealed that the discussion group was treated as an avant garde phenomenon. Obviously, discussion dates back at least to Socrates' time. The seminar was well established in the college curriculum long before there was widespread interest in the discussion method. However, a look at the typical seminar may be instructive.

Usually there is a requirement that each member present on some aspect of the course. Members therefore tend to focus their attention and energies on the area in which they are to present. Consequently, they tend to listen selectively to the presentations of others with the hope that they can shine in the group by diverting the discussion to their own area of expertise. At the conclusion of a presentation, it is not uncommon to hear a response that goes something like this: 'That was a quite adequate presentation, however, I feel that more might have been said about X.' X is of course the respondent's assigned area. This is recognized immediately by the reader as Seminarmanship. This particular ploy accomplishes two objectives in the one statement: namely, puts the presenter down, gently of course, and diverts the discussion to the area where the respondent can shine. Other Seminarmanship lore worth mentioning is the role of maintaining the status quo. If anyone in the group seems to be in need of help, either ignore his cry for assistance or throw him an anchor. After all, someone has to get the C's and D's, and once a member's ignorance has been exposed, it is best to let the chips (or grades) fall where they may. A corollary of this is never to indicate to the instructor that you have learned anything from the group discussion—again, this might rebound against you. There are ploys too numerous to mention in how to be one up in a seminar, but the brief coverage here may suffice to indicate the grave insufficiency of the typical seminar as a vehicle for learning.

Before dealing with this method, let us first examine the relationship between the student and the learning process, with a view towards discovering the requirements that a discussion group must meet to provide learning for the student. A student learns and passes his examinations by doing homework and class work. Usually the former requires silent studying of the text, and the latter involves attending lectures. In Learning Thru Discussion (LTD) the student must do his homework, which means reading the assignment. This cannot be postponed to the night before the examination but must be done prior to each and every group discussion period. Admittedly, discussion can go on without preparation, and, in fact, ignorance of the topic facilitates the development of heated discussions. The only trouble is that there is more heat generated than light.

Preparation for discussion in LTD makes special homework demands and will be covered in detail later in this manual.

How one learns about a subject in the lecture situation is self-evident, but how anyone learns in the discussion situation is a bit of a mystery to most students. A logical analysis of a group where the students come prepared reveals four possible conditions under which a student could be classified.

First of all, a student may have prepared his assignment and had no trouble understanding a particular topic. This we will call condition A. On the other hand, a student might not understand a particular topic—condition B. In the discussion group, it might happen that for a particular topic condition A prevails, i.e., everyone understands it. Groups often dwell at length on topics which everyone understands and they 'beat it to death.' The security operation is of course dominant and no learning takes place. The *LTD* method suggests, as we shall see, that the group bypass topics in which Condition A prevails. Similarly, it may happen that Condition B is prevalent and no one understands the topic. This does not necessarily inhibit discussion, and in fact, some of the most animated interaction takes place when no one knows what they are talking about. Again, however, no learning is taking place. The *LTD* method suggests that under this circumstance the resource expert or the text be consulted or, failing this, the group move on. The above recommendations for conditions A and B indicate how learning groups can be efficient.

Usually, in a group, a mixed condition obtains. We do not have all A's or all B's but some of each. This is the true learning situation, and, for learning to take place, it is necessary for those who don't understand (B) to communicate this; and for those who do understand (A) to respond in kind. For different topics we would expect different people in the groups to occupy the A and B roles.

When this interaction prescription is in operation, we can see how information is shared and knowledge is disseminated throughout the group. It is clear how the B's have benefited— but how about the A's? When the A's and B's interact, two new categories emerge. Everyone has had the experience of trying to explain something to another person and realizing that his understanding is incomplete, hence condition C—not fully understanding that which you think you understand. This is perhaps the most crucial aspect for learning in the discussion group. In the group situation, it is possible to play the teaching role and as the old saying goes, you never really learn a subject until you teach it. Quite possibly one of the strengths of the old-fashioned one-room school house was that it was necessary that students in higher grades assist in the instruction of the children in the lower grades. There has been much current emphasis by Thelen and others in placing students in teaching roles as part of their educational development.

To complete the logical analysis, there is a fourth type emerging from the interaction of so-called A's and B's— namely the person who thinks he doesn't understand a topic but in reality does—condition D. This occurs when someone explains what it is they don't understand and in formulating the question perceives the answer. This is sometimes called thinking out loud.

Thus, we have learning taking place, according to this formal analysis, through the interaction of the A's and B's and the generating of two new types—C's and D's. It is not too difficult, therefore, to see, structurally, the potential for learning that exists in a group.

However, students often have great verbal facility and can drop names and concepts with the greatest of ease and yet not have real understanding of the basic facts. The logical analysis offered above does not deal with pseudo-learning, and LTD, while it does take advantage of the group potential, also introduces procedures to minimize the so-called pseudo-learning that abounds in education. In particular, the Group Cognitive Map, to be discussed in the next chapter, places strong emphasis on learning exactly what the author has to say on a subject.

Another advantage of this method is that in helping each other, the students, are communicating at about the same level, whereas the instructor may be going over their heads. Also, students often have the frustrating experience of not understanding some aspect of the course and being unable to state the source of their difficulty. Other students who approach the material from the same disadvantage point can often diagnose the nature of a fellow student's difficulty much better than the instructor.

In the development of the *LTD* method, two considerations were uppermost; an appreciation of the method requires an understanding of the operation of these two fundamental conceptions. First, it must be kept in mind that a discussion group is a group and is, therefore, subject to the canons of group development and group dynamics. This obvious fact has apparently been overlooked by the didactically oriented discussion leader. Group interaction inevitably generates communication problems but it also exposes new potentials for learning; a method of group discussion should try to minimize the effect of these problems and maximize the group potential. Second, it must be kept in mind that this group-oriented consideration must not obscure the particular purpose of subject matter mastery. This obvious fact has apparently been overlooked by the group-oriented discussion leader. His goal is the development of a 'good' group, and the learning of the lesson becomes almost incidental. In such cases the definition of a good group is vague, high-sounding, and indisputable. It is indisputable because it is idealistic and untestable. If we pursue the considerations underlying the method, then a good group can be defined in more specific terms. A good group is one where the process, or communication, problems are adequately handled and the potential of the members realized, so that the learning of the course material is enhanced. *LTD* is designed to encompass the foregoing considerations, and the method consists of three parts: the Group Cognitive Map, Group Roles and Member Skills, and the List of Criteria. These are interrelated but must, perforce, be dealt with individually.

GROUP COGNITIVE MAP

AS HAS ALREADY been indicated, group discussions are often characterized by lack of direction, and the topics that are discussed arise fortuitously or at the insistence of a dominating member with the compliance of submissive, indifferent, or confused members. No one knows what behavior is appropriate to the situation or, if they think they do, they cannot be sure that anyone else would agree with them. Appropriate behavior actually consists of developing some procedure for adequately discussing the material. A poor plan that is endorsed and followed by all the members is better than none at all. Certainly, what is desirable is a program that logically relates to the goal of learning. The group Cognitive Map is a procedural tool which outlines an orderly sequence that a group should follow in order to learn from discussion. It is the instructor's job to present this map to the group and to explain its significance and operation. For the Group Cognitive Map to be effective, a mandate must be derived from the group so that it can be put into operation with the consent and active support of the members. Once this is accomplished the group has a *shared* and agreed-upon method of proceeding. For a great many reasons, there will be both overt and covert resistance to accepting the Group Cognitive Map. The instructor must assert his prerogative to conduct the discussion group along the lines he thinks best.

The Group Cognitive Map is made up of nine steps which are presented here in tabular form. The rationale and behavior for each step will be dealt with in detail immediately following the tabulation. We assume the existence of suitable study materials, available to all, and read prior to the meeting.

GROUP COGNITIVE MAP

Step One   –   Definition of terms and concepts

Step Two   –   General statement of author's message

Step Three   –   Identification of major themes or sub-
                  topics

Step Four   –   Allocation of time

Step Five   –   Discussion of major themes and subtopics

Step Six   –   Integration of material with other knowledge

Step Seven   –   Application of the material

Step Eight   –   Evaluation of author's presentation

Step Nine   –   Evaluation of group and individual
                  performance

Step One – Definition of Terms and Concepts

One objective of the Group Cognitive Map is to lessen the possibility of the group's becoming involved in useless argument. It is now standard operating procedure to define terms before discussing any subject. This avoids the so-called semantic trap which ensnares so many groups. Also, the act of defining terms in itself constitutes learning. In introductory courses, mastering the technical language is often half the course, and where objective tests are used, covers half the examination. Consequently, in some courses considerable time might legitimately be spent on this step. One pitfall is the tendency for a student to extend the definition of a term into a resume of the whole assignment. The instructor will probably have to indicate what is appropriate for this step. In reading technical and scientific material, it is often necessary to consult dictionaries specific to the field under consideration. Most students have to be told that Webster's is not infallible and that for certain terms it can be either unrewarding or misleading. Often the instructor has to make such technical and scientific dictionaries available.

Step Two — General Statement of Author's Message

The purpose of this step is to obtain some grasp of the overall meaning of the assigned reading. Enunciation of a general statement should accomplish this. It also demarcates the area to be discussed, that is, it zeros in on the topic for discussion. It also serves the purpose of launching the discussion. Some authors, particularly of text books, begin each chapter with a clearly designated general statement which greatly simplifies the student's task and thereby lessens the time spent in this step. Even so, the members should state the general purpose of the assignment in their own words. Quite often the task is not so simple, and the determination of the author's main point is no small intellectual accomplishment. In these circumstances the formulation of the author's overall message may in itself constitute important learning and may also greatly facilitate the task to be encountered in Step Three.

Step Three — Identification of Major Themes of Subtopics

Most material can be broken down into a number of important subtopics. Again, authors of text books not only organize their material in this fashion but even provide sub-headings. Although most of the job is thereby done for the student, these subtopics should be restated in the student's own words to assure his understanding. In other cases, a close analysis of the material is required to isolate and enunciate the subtopics, and usually much is learned in the pursuit of this task. It should be apparent that in *LTD* great emphasis is placed on determining what the author has to say, rather than on the opinions of the students.

Step Four — Allocation of Time

This is a crucial step in the method. The common complaint of discussion-group members is that they never cover the material and spend too much time on one aspect to the neglect of all the rest. To meet this real difficulty the group must budget its time, and conduct the discussion accordingly. Actually, there is never enough time in a group any more than there is in life, to accomplish everything, no matter how well budgeted the available time may be. This is particularly true in this case, when one considers that time must be made available, not only for the topics isolated in Step Three, but also to fulfill the requirements of Steps Five, Six, Seven, Eight, and Nine. The value of Step Four lies in the fact that the group sets its own time limits and, as a group, gains some grasp of the area to be discussed and can thereby regulate itself accordingly. The results obtained by omitting this step are not hard to visualize; in fact all readers have had unfortunate experiences with groups that had no regulatory clock and could not pace themselves appropriately. While this step is crucial, it is also the most difficult one of all the groups to master. There are many obvious reasons for this. One invalid type of reasoning is 'Since there is little enough time as it is, why use some of it up deciding about how much time is to be spent on each topic?' This would be valid if a group were heroically attempting to cover all the material. In *LTD* method this is considered wasteful, and the discussion period should be used to deal with only those parts of the material that the members, for one reason or another, feel it would be most profitable to discuss. Usually some of the assigned reading is readily understood and need not be recapitulated. Learning to exercise this selectivity is not easy, and, at the outset, groups have difficulty in determining, with any degree of confidence, what needs and does not need discussion. Sometimes, the least understood parts are nominated for exclusion in order to avoid the embarrassment of exposing ignorance, and a group will prefer to discuss that which is already known. Also, the group cannot estimate accurately how much time is needed in Steps Five, Six, Seven, Eight, and Nine until it has had some experience with the method. The instructor must be prepared for the group's having difficulty with this step and encourage it to persevere.

Step Five – Discussion of Major Themes and Subtopics

It is important to note that so far in the *LTD* method there has been no acutal discussion of the assignment, only a clearing away and tooling up for the discussion! The discussion should proceed within the strictures laid down in Step Four, wherein the topics have been selected and time and priority have been allocated. As might be anticipated, groups will become frustrated with their inability to carry out their own decisions in regard to allocation of time, and this will negatively affect the quality of the discussion. What is to be done in this step is clear, but it is more easily explained than executed. The *LTD* method does not create these problems; it only makes the group aware of them.

In this step, as in Steps Two and Three, the emphasis is still on the author's message and not on the personal opinions of the group members. As has been emphasized, any expression of the personal reactions of members has so far been forbidden by the method. This is not because these are thought to be of no significance. Quite the contrary, it is only that we have found in our experience that groups never discover what the author has to say if they begin by giving their personal opinions. Inevitably this leads to diversions or disagreement. Sides are drawn up, and what the author has to say is of only incidental importance. Thus, in *LTD* the expression of personal reactions is postponed until the group has discussed the text. The idea of being acquainted with what authorities in a field actually say is, in itself, a novel development in many discussion circles. For example, most people have very decided opinions on evolution, psychoanalysis, and communism and yet have read little or nothing by Darwin, Freud, or Marx. *LTD* is intended to counteract this condition, but the instructor will find resistance to a method which curbs the members' self-expression. He must try to get the group members to channel these personal observations into Step Eight. This requires delay of gratification, which is usually considered a mark of maturity, and therefore cannot be expected to be readily practiced early in the life of a group. The demand for self-expression and the inability of the group to complete the discussion of a topic within the alloted time will be the two main problems encountered in this step.

Step Six — Integration of the Material

An oft-heard criticism of the educational system is that learning is too fragmentary and too much concerned with the acquisition of isolated bits of information. The use of multiple choice and true-false examinations reinforces this kind of learning. It is a well-known fact of learning theory that isolated, unassociated facts are the first to be forgotten. Even if they are retained, they may still be unattached to any body of knowledge and are therefore of limited value.

To counteract this possibility, *LTD* requires group members to allocate time and make a conscious effort to relate learnings in the assignment to ideas and concepts acquired in previous meetings or other learning situations. If this is carried out successfully, over a period of time a student should amass a body of knowledge that would be more integrated and more likely to be retained.

Again, we may find that in introductory courses the student feels he does not have much to interrelate. As the course proceeds, this step may come to have a more important function. In some advanced courses this may well be the most vital of all the steps, and proportionately more time would be devoted to it. At the outset, an instructor may have to provide examples of cross-referencing and integrating in order for the student to grasp the cognitive task appropriate to this step.

Step Seven — Application of the Material

The criticism of the educational system raised above occurs again here in a slightly altered form. Knowledge should not only be accumulative and integrated, but it also should have personal value or significance for the student. Subject matter mastery should enhance feelings of ego mastery. Acquired knowledge that is not internalized and remains ego-alien is either readily forgotten, or results in the creation of arid scholasticism or mere pedantry. The reader is invited to conjecture on the extent to which learning in our schools and colleges is unintegrated and meaningless to the student.

To counteract this likelihood, *LTD* requires group members to allocate time and make a conscious effort to assess the possible applications and implications of the material. Some subjects, e.g., psychology, often have very direct personal application. Others may have less personal application, but many implications of an intellectual nature that the student can develop. Again, in introductory courses the students usually have difficulty in seeing the relevance of the lesson, and the instructor, may at the outset, have to provide the group with appropriate examples.

Step Eight — Evaluation of the Author's Presentation

At long last, the personal reactions of the student are programmed into the method. The rationale for this postponement has already been given. In addition, it is often the case that after covering the other steps, the students' criticism has less affective loading and becomes more constructive. From group-work theory, we know that affective reactions will out, and the method should not be used to squelch them, but only to provide an appropriate time and place for their expression and also, hopefully, to encourage their outlet in a more goal-directed and sublimated form. A particularly turgid piece of writing can be very frustrating, and the student has every right to give vent to his feelings of frustration. If learning is to be served, however, criticism should become critique and, rather than being eliminated, should be raised to a level of incisiveness. The development of the ability to think critically may well be more important than the learning of the material itself, as it will serve the student well in all future learning and life situations. Consequently, if this step can be something in addition to affective unloading, namely the development of the critical faculty, this may well be the greatest accomplishment of the method.

The development of the ability to evaluate reading assignments does not come as easily as the rendering of affective reactions, and students usually will require from thc instructor many examples before they feel competent to perform this task.

Step Nine — Evaluation of Group and Individual Performance

For the method to work, this step is essential. As a matter of fact, for any group to be effective some time must be devoted to evaluating the inevitable individual problems and group process problems. In the *LTD* method it is suggested that approximately the last ten minutes of the hour be devoted to diagnosing and evaluating the group and individual effectiveness. Many well-trained group leaders would insist on dealing with group problems as they are manifested, rather than handling them at a specific time. That they *are* handled is more important than *when* they are handled. Both on-the-spot and scheduled approaches have been used without any evidence indicating which one is better. The only point that can be made is that the logic of the method suggests that evaluation should be set aside as a separate step and that the group budget time for it. On-the-spot inquiries have the advantage of immediacy, but also have the disadvantage of preventing the group from staying within its self-imposed time budget, thereby providng an alibi for its shortcomings. A group will invariably find difficulty in ultilizing the Group Cognitive Map when it is starting out, and it should be forced to face up to this and overcome it. Otherwise the method will always be frustrating and self-defeating.

As this step is so important and also so specialized, it will be dealt with separately and at some length after the Group Cognitive Map, Group Roles and Member Skills, and the List of Criteria have been covered. At this point it can be mentioned that while the analysis of individual role and group process problems is highly specialized, the *LTD* method is designed to greatly simplify the task. Again, the instructor can be helpful by example, sharing his diagnosis, insights, and interpretations of what is occurring in this group. This will give the group members a model to follow. This, too, will be dealt with more fully in a section covering the responsibilities of the instructor.

All groups generate both individual and group problems and the added requirement of mastering the Group Cognitive Map makes it necessary that time be devoted to this step. As a group develops, however, it should not need to compulsively go through the motions expected in Step Nine, but only use it from time to time as needed.

A final word on the Group Cognitive Map. The technique should be used appropriately and creatively, which means that the allotment of time to the steps should vary for different groups, subjects, and course goals. The disbursement of the sequence of steps may be varied for a particular group as it develops. Furthermore, the steps may be altered to meet idiosyncratic conditions, and the Group Cognitive Map reported here is intended more as a general plan and guide for the instructor or group member. The instructor should assess the nature of the material, his course objectives, the kind of student he will be dealing with and formulate his own version of the Group Cognitive Map, before the group meets.

The term 'group cognitive map,' was introduced by Coffey in programming a logical sequence of steps for problem-solving groups. The term, 'cognitive map,' was borrowed from Tolman, who used it in his learning theories to explain the behavior of rats running mazes. Learning to use the Group Cognitive Map may invite an unflattering parallel with learning to run a maze. The parallel diverges only when there is added to this structure the function of the other two parts of the *LTD* method—The Group Roles and Member Skills, and the List of Criteria.

GROUP ROLES AND MEMBER SKILLS

EARLIER, IT WAS STATED that for a discussion to be successful there must be recognition that it is a *group* and principles of group work should apply. One important principle is that certain roles have to be performed and members must have the interpersonal skill to perform them. Ever since K. D. Benne's and P. Sheats's original article on group roles ('Functional Roles of Group Members,' *Journal of Social Issues,* vol. 4 no. 2, 1948), workshops and laboratories in human relations training have been developing lists of group roles. No complete or final list can be prepared, and the one presented here is not exhaustive but selective. The selection has been guided by the learning theory implicit in *LTD* as well as by group theory.

Group roles are usually classified as 'group maintenance,' or 'task accomplishment,' or both. This distinction is observed in our organization of group roles. In it we have followed the standard nomenclature found in group-work literature. Usually there is much overlap and repetition, and this has been deliberately minimized by grouping the overlapping roles into three functional clusters:

A. Sequence of task roles specific to discussion of a topic,
B. Overall task roles required in the *LTD* method,
C. Group maintenance roles required in the *LTD* method.

Before presenting in tabular form the list of roles and a detailed description of each, a few words of caution about role theory is indicated. Group roles, in amended form, were previously leader roles; with the democratization of the group, members must assume the responsibilities that leaders were presumed to carry out. In the assumption of this responsibility it is best not to have a simple division of labor with one role for each member. An effective group member can and should perform many, if not all, the group roles with some finesse. A member playing any one role consistently and persistently will be more of a hindrance than a help. There is a concept of appropriateness inherent in the exercise of group roles and a need for member sensitivity is indicated.

GROUP ROLES AND MEMBER SKILLS

A. Sequence of task roles specific to discussion of a topic

    1. Initiating
    2. Giving and asking for information
    3. Giving and asking for reactions
    4. Restating and giving examples
    5. Confronting and reality testing
    6. Clarifying, synthesizing, and summarizing

B. Overall task roles required in *Learning Thru Discussion* method

    7. Gatekeeping and expediting
    8. Timekeeping
    9. Evaluating and diagnosing
    10. Standard setting

C. Group maintenance roles required in *Learning Thru Discussion* method

    11. Sponsoring and encouraging
    12. Group tension relieving

A. Sequence of Task Roles Specific to Discussion of a Topic

1. *Initiating.* Sometimes a group has trouble getting started or resuming discussion when a lull falls upon it. Apparently each member is waiting for someone else to get the group going. Anyone *can* break the sound barrier, but someone *must.* The basis for reluctance to perform this routine service, like the resistance to performing any task or maintenance role, often lies in a member's unwillingness to be perceived and rejected as an aspiring leader. Resistance to getting down to work is also common to the performance of these roles.

2. *Giving and asking for information.* In the *LTD* method, students are required to state the general message and the ideas contained in the subtopics. In a well-developed group this information will be readily volunteered, but in beginning groups it may have to be solicited. The members must share their understandings of the material freely or else the discussion will be awkward and stilted.

3. *Giving and asking for reactions.* When a member does share his understanding of a point, groups often treat it as a curtain closer and remain silent or move on without comment. For learning to take place some reaction should be volunteered or solicited. In some groups there is no interaction; instead there is a rotation process, and one member states his understanding of a topic and passes it on to the member on his right who gives his understanding on the next topic and so on. This type of group ritual accomplishes little learning since no one is listening, but reciting to himself the offering he will render when it comes around' to his turn. Usually, but not always, explanations by one member merit or could be enhanced by reactions from others. If there is no feedback, the members are not going to get much more out of the discussion than they could obtain from silent reading.

4. *Restating and giving examples.* This is usually a specific type of 3, giving and asking for reactions. If a member restates what another has said, he provides feedback to the original speaker. By restating he provides a test of whether the member accurately communicated what he intended. The value of giving examples cannot be overemphasized. A good example illuminates for all the meaning of what is being said in a way that no amount of elaboration can accomplish.

5. *Confronting and reality testing.* This is involved in 3, giving and asking for reactions and 4, restating and giving examples. Certainly one form of reality testing is to restate in your own words what someone else has just said. This provides a test of communication and of the correctness of the idea in the message. Many groups allow misinformation and misstatements to pass by. Allegedly, this is done in order not to embarrass the speaker; actually it is to save themselves embarrassment. Confronting is an important function if learning is to take place. Suggesting that someone else's statement is not entirely accurate requires skill and ego strength.

6. *Clarifying, synthesizing, and summarizing.* Even with the simplest of material, groups can get into complicated tangles and are, from time to time, in great need of someone to play the clarifying role. Also, where a number of restatements of a topic have been made, for example, synthesis is needed. Clarifying and synthesizing have the value of providing closure, as does summarizing, and allowing the group to move on to the next item on the agenda.

B. Overall Task Roles Required in Learning Thru Discussion

7. *Gatekeeping and expediting.* One of the most common behaviors in fulfilling this role involves attempts to spread

participation. A typical gatekeeping remark is, "We haven't heard from X; what do you think about . . . ?" Gatekeeping, or expediting, is directly connected with holding the group to the Group Cognitive Map and moving it through its steps.

8. *Timekeeping.* This is a specific instance of 7, gatekeeping and expediting, and is of particular importance in the *LTD* method. If a group is to keep within its time budget, someone must keep an eye on the clock, at least until the group learns to pace itself automatically. It is desirable for members to become involved, but this often means neglect of the budgeted time for a topic, and if this role is neglected, the group may not pass through all the phases of the discussion.

9. *Evaluating and diagnosing.* In the Group Cognitive Map, evaluation and diagnosis is deferred until Step Nine, and then it is expected that most, if not all, will participate. Even when this procedure is adhered to, members need to silently fill this role during the ongoing discussion or else there will be little to bring up when Step Nine is reached. One technique that has been successfully used is to assign one member to be the process observer, and he makes a report, at Step Nine, of the observations he has garnered throughout the discussion. Some training and experience is required to fulfill this role, but checking against the requirements of the Group Cognitive Map, Group Roles and Member Skills, and the List of Criteria (to be discussed in the next section) is sufficient for understanding most group problems.

10. *Standard Setting.* This is sometimes called the group's 'ego ideal,' and the role requirement is to indicate to the group the standards of performance that they have implicitly or explicitly set for themselves. This role should be activated when there is a wide discrepancy between current performance and group standards. The next section, the List of

Criteria, sets forth explicitly the standards required by the *LTD* method; operation in this role will be more readily understood if this section is consulted. *LTD* suggests that this role and 9, evaluating and diagnosing, be exercised in Step Nine of the Group Cognitive Map, but, as stated earlier, there is no evidence at this time to indicate that on-the-spot use of these roles is contraindicated.

11. *Sponsoring and Encouraging.* Roles 1, initiating, and 7, gatekeeping and expediting, are specific examples. Certain members need sponsoring from time to time and all members need encouragement. The encouraging remark is not only important to the recipient, but it also tends to contribute to a warm and accepting climate which in turn encourages voluntary participation. The giving of praise or encouragement seems to be alien to our culture. Because of this, students need encouragement in performing the encouraging role. Skill, as well as ego strength, is required in drawing out silent members. Inept performance of this role can have the opposite effect of that intended and can intrench a member in this nonparticipant behavior.

12. *Group Tension Relieving.* A role that might be likened to a thermostat should be available which will be activated when tensions get too high. When discussions become deadly serious, or frustration over following the Group Cognitive Map, becomes unbearable, or disagreements about the meaning of the material become intense, the thermostat should activate this tension-relieving role. Behaviors associated with the role are kidding, telling jokes, and making diverting and off-target remarks. Sometimes this role is referred to in the literature as harmonizing. It is worth noting that behaviors associated with this role are considered to be nonfunctional and disruptive when they are not in the service of group maintenance.

In the treatment of this topic, the nonfunctional roles are usually described in detail. While they are disruptive to the goals of the *LTD* method, there is nothing of a special quality introduced by the method. They are therefore listed without comment. If the reader does not find the roles to be self-evident from their titles, he can consult Benne and Sheats for further elucidation.

NONFUNCTIONAL ROLES

1. Aggressing
2. Blocking
3. Self-confessing
4. Competing
5. Seeking sympathy
6. Special interest pleader
7. Horsing around (playboy)
8. Status seeking
9. Withdrawing
10. Dominating

One role not included in the regular list of Group Roles and of particular importance in the *LTD* method is listening. The magazine supplements of the Sunday newspapers invariably have an article on the importance of being a good listener. Apparently if this role is completely mastered, all your ambitions will be realized. Our claims are more modest. Good listening will promote good interaction and learning. The distinction to be made is between active and passive listening. If members are actively listening their chances of learning something are greatly improved. If their 'hearing aid' is turned down, not only will they not learn anything, but they will have a very depressing effect on the participating members.

The significance of Group Roles should now be apparent. If many of these roles are missing from the discussion, it will inevitably bog down, and the learning potential of the discussion group will not be realized.

LIST OF CRITERIA FOR A GOOD GROUP

A NUMBER OF PROBLEMS connected with the use of the discussion group have been propounded. Perhaps, as with your Friendly Finance Company, all of these problems can be consolidated into one big problem! The overall problem is the inexperience of the typical student with the discussion method. The typical student, because of years of academic exposure, knows all too well what is expected of him and what he can expect from the traditional lecture situation. He has no similar set of expectations when confronted with the group discussion approach. This problem is compounded by the fact that not only is his previous academic experience of little help, but also his other experiences with formal groups have in all probability not been too satisfying. Thus even the most highly motivated student has difficulty being effective, because he has no model of a good group nor a clear image of the kind of behavior that would contribute to building one. Consequently, what is needed is a concept of what a good group should be, and this concept should be shared by all the group members. Goal-directed behavior cannot be achieved in the absence of shared goals.

The instructor's task therefore would be to help the group members to formulate some concept of what constitutes a good group learning situation. Much of what has already been said in the sections on the Group Cognitive Map and on Group Roles and Member Skills points to the requirements for an effective democratically oriented discussion group. A group must have some notion of how it should operate, some standard of performance, or, in our terms, a list of criteria. The criteria function as a goal and also as a standard against which to measure current performance.

A list of criteria is presented here which is not by any means exhaustive, but is intended to cover the major conditions that are required for the efficient operation of the *LTD* method. All groups should be encouraged to add to this list as their experience dictates. The criteria are presented here in tabular form, and then each is discussed in detail.

LIST OF CRITERIA

1. Prevalence of a warm, accepting, nonthreatening group climate.
2. Learning is approached as a cooperative enterprise.
3. Learning is accepted as the raison d'être of the group.
4. Everyone participates and interacts.
5. Leadership functions are distributed.
6. Group sessions and the learning task are enjoyable.
7. The material is adequately and efficiently covered.
8. Evaluation is accepted as an integral part of the group operation.
9. Members attend regularly and come prepared.

1. *Prevalence of a warm, accepting, nonthreatening group climate.* In the last few years there has been an impressive number of studies reported in education literature attesting to the value for learning of nonthreatening classroom environment. A climate of acceptance is an important factor in any learning situation. It is of particular importance in the *LTD* method, which requires a student to expose his ignorance,

confront his fellow students and in other ways dissolve his interpersonal defenses. This kind of behavior will be attempted only in a warm and accepting climate. Most of the points made in the ensuing criteria assume the operation of such a group climate.

2. *Learning is approached as a cooperative enterprise.* Students reared in the traditional academic manner unconsciously accept the idea that the competitive orientation is the *only* way to succeed. Aggressiveness, one-upmanship, attempts to impress, status seeking, and competitive behavior are seen as dysfunctional in the *LTD* method. For instance, many students have come to believe that if they have nothing brilliant or witty to say, they had better remain silent, and they usually do. Rewards and approbation must be given to cooperative behavior. The learner, not the learned, is the good group member. Asking for help in understanding promotes understanding for all.

3. *Learning is accepted as the raison d'être of the group.* The point of having a discussion group is to promote learning. This is obvious, but in a cohesive group it can become obscurred. In some groups, members may become so enamored with the cohesiveness of the group that the goals of the group may become obscured. Because of the relative rarity in our society of satisfactory group experiences, there will be a tendency for members to use such an opportunity, when it does arise, unduly, to satisfy legitimate interpersonal needs.

4. *Everyone participates and interacts.* A group in which only a few members participate is obviously not a good group. On the other hand, it is not possible to have participation meted out into absolutely equal shares. Nevertheless, all members should participate some of the time. If a member

does not participate, he may not be getting much from the group; but what is more important, he certainly isn't contributing anything to the group. When silent members are questioned about their lack of participation, they characteristically respond, with a note of virtue in their voices, that while they may not be participating, they are getting a lot out of the discussion, and that they remain silent so that the better informed members can give the group the benefit of their wisdom. The *LTD* method needs for its successful operation the contribution of *all* group members and particularly of those who do not fully comprehend. If we hear only from those who 'know,' then it would be more efficient to get 'the word' from the instructor in the first place.

By interaction is meant the reacting of members to each other. Participation is differentiated from interaction, even though interaction is dependent on participation, because it is possible to have high participation and low interaction concurrently. For example, in groups where each member takes his turn in reciting from the assignment, there is little attention paid to the current speaker since his audience is not listening, but silently rehearsing. If there is little interaction, there is also little learning.

5. *Leadership functions are distributed.* Responsibility for making the group operate should not be delegated to or usurped by one or a few members. The Group Roles discussed in the previous section must be performed in order for the group to function adequately and for learning to take place. If all the members are going to learn, they must all participate, interact, and perform leadership functions.

6. *Group sessions and the learning task are enjoyable.* While mottoes like 'learning can be fun' repel the sophisticated reader, something needs to be said on the subject since this rather detailed analysis of discussion groups may have

suggested to the reader that a group is to perform in a very serious fashion. Group discussion is not meant to be a grim business. Quite the contrary! Some frustration will inevitably be encountered in the beginning, but the result intended is for learning to become rewarding, satisfying, and even exciting. When the members are grimly and methodically trying to learn, something is wrong with the operation, and evaluation of the process is in order.

7. *The material is adequately and efficiently covered.* The significance of this point for learning is self-evident and well labored in the section on the Group Cognitive Map.

8. *Evaluation is accepted as an integral part of the group operation.* A good group is one that accepts the inevitability of encountering problems and is willing to evaluate its progress. Perhaps enough has been said on evaluation, but even with groups that fully accept the foregoing statements this step is frequently bypassed. The reason for this bit of cognitive dissonance is that a group gets caught in a vicious circle. If all goes well in a group, there is time for evaluation, but little need for it. If the group gets into difficulties, it needs evaluation, but, seemingly, has little time for it, because the problem itself is time consuming. In short, the paradox is that when a group has no time for evaluation, it probably needs it most. The instructor must insist on group evaluation.

9. *Members attend regularly and come prepared.* Any small group is demoralized and rendered ineffective by the irregular attendance of group members. Besides problems of continuity, the members who do come secretly feel foolish and resentful at being party to what is apparently considered by some as not worth the effort. If members come unprepared, the *LTD* method absolutely will *not* work. Unprepared members can get something out of attending, but they are

parasitic to the life of the group. Also they can be quite detrimental if they insist in bluffing their way through. There must be a group standard that members attend regularly and come prepared. If the latter standard is not met, there should be an auxillary standard requiring the unprepared members to keep quiet.

HOW TO MAKE LTD WORK

MANY STATEMENTS have been made throughout the text on the roles and responsibilities of the instructor and the members. The foregoing remarks can be summarized by saying that both the instructor and student are responsible for behaving in ways that will hold the group to the Group Cognitive Map and will fulfill the Group Roles and meet the List of Criteria. In this section we will not repeat what was previously said, but will attempt to place the instructor and the members in their proper relationship to the *LTD* method.

Role of the Instructor

There are two roles the instructor plays in the group. One concerns subject matter and the other group performance. These will be taken up in order.

The quality of learning is obviously limited by the quality of the materials used in the course. As in any course, the instructor must select carefully the text or readings. It sometimes happens that the instructor feels that there is no adequate text in the field, and he must therefore cover the subject through his lectures. In such instances he should write out his lectures. duplicate them, and make them available in advance to the class.

During class periods, one role the instructor assumes is technically called resource expert. In this role he should not rescue the group every time they encounter difficulty, if they are to learn to think for themselves. There are occasions, however, when they do not have the background to resolve their confusion, and the text is not of much help. On these occasions the group should call on the resource expert. This task is more difficult to perform in large classes which are broken down into several small discussion groups.

Usually he will circulate from group to group and be available if needed. Another technique is to hold meetings of the entire class once a week and answer questions that have originated in the small group discussions.

Another role that the instructor plays in the class is technically termed group trainer. Because of the students' lack of familiarity with learning in discussion groups and with the *LTD* method, the instructor must do some training of the members of his class. The first item of business is to acquaint the students with the mechanics of the Group Cognitive Map, the Group Roles and Member Skills, and the List of Criteria. This manual, hopefully, will lessen the burden, particularly if each member has a copy.

Once the group is launched, the training role alters and also becomes fused with the resource expert role. As the meetings are to be conducted democratically, the instructor should participate minimally. His main job is to observe how the group is progressing with the *LTD* method. He then feeds back his observations to the group and may offer suggestions for overcoming difficulties that the members have encountered. In large classes some variation has to be made. Visiting the small groups, noting their difficulties, and then reporting the observations to the reassembled total group has worked in practice. Another variation is for each small group to appoint

its own process observer to make notes on the group operation, while abstaining from the discussion. The process observ-
ers then make brief reports to the total group. The fact that
each of the small groups discuss the same material and have
approximately the same difficulties results in the report from
a process observer being of value to all the class. This technique of course does not preclude observations and interpretations on the part of the instructor. A byproduct of this
technique is the value that the process observer derives from
the experience. He usually gets a much clearer perspective of
the *LTD* method in action than any amount of instruction
could provide. If this technique is employed, it is suggested
that the process observer role be rotated.

An instructor should approach the training job creatively.
He should devise his own variations of the method and experi-
ment with different approaches in order to improve it. Variations have been tried, and a number of tricks of the trade
have been evolved. Some of these techniques are adaptations
made by previous instructors and may be of some help to
prospective ones.

1. In introducing a class to the method, it is usual to give
a brief explanation of the need for structure in group discussion and explain the three elements of *LTD* (Group Cognitive
Map, Group and Member Roles, and List of Criteria) and how
it aids in solving problems inherent in group discussion. Such
a classroom presentation has been video taped and is available
from the author. This presentation, by Dr. Hill and Dr.
Stoller, is 16 mm., black and white, has a sound track, and
runs thirty minutes. Also, in our mode of operation it is
required that all participants acquire a copy of this book and
read it prior to the first discussion session.

2. Conduct a demonstration group in which the instructor
assumes responsibility for moving the group through the *LTD*
steps.

3. Designate a leader from the group who will assume
responsibility for getting the group to follow the *LTD*

method. His job would be procedural rather than didactic. As in the case of the process observer, a designated leader learns a great deal about the operation of the method and usually becomes a better group member. Consequently, this duty should be rotated so that all members have the opportunity to be designated leaders. This has been found to be quite successful in activating nonparticipating members. When the *LTD* method is fairly well assimilated there should be no need for a designated leader.

4. In preparing for the discussion, the student is required to make out preparation sheets. These will be discussed in the immediately following subsection. In aiding and reinforcing this operation, the instructor might make out a model preparation sheet and circulate it as a guide. Or he might have them handed in and corrected and returned. Also, the preparation sheets could be graded and contribute to the determination of the student's final grade in the class. When a level of proficiency has been obtained for the preparation sheets, grades could be assigned on the basis of class contribution.

5. Initial meetings might deal with easier material, and the group could practice on subject matter that was not of crucial importance.

6. Experience suggests a ground rule by which the group members are not to open their texts during the discussion, although they may make references to the preparation sheets. Otherwise, students bury themselves in the text, and interaction suffers drastically. It could be permissable to consult the text only for points of fact.

7. The list of Group Roles can be converted into a rating sheet, and the members can rate themselves, each other, or the group, as to the frequency with which various roles are performed. Just the act of filling out the rating sheet may sensitize members to weaknesses in their own performance. In large classes composed of several subgroups, having these filled out from time to time may provide the instructor with some

check on the groups. Similarly, some sort of postmeeting reaction sheet on which the students check or otherwise indicate their reactions and evaluations of the group meetings can be useful (see appendix).

Usually we have the members fill out the postmeeting reaction sheets before we begin our Step Nine discussion. Also, we ask the designated leader to tally the postmeeting reaction sheet responses and feed them back to the group, indicating the percentage of responses in each category. When these are accumulated, so that the group can see how the ratings have shifted over a span of several meetings, this often leads to some insightful discussions of the group and its problems.

One final word to the instructor. The *LTD* method will work only if the instructor is firm in his demand that the group follow the method.

Role of the Student

Very simply restated, the role of the student in the *LTD* method requires that he internalize and implement the Group Cognitive Map and that he play most of the group roles and that he tries to make his behavior consistent with the criteria. In particular, there are five interaction behaviors which he should practice.

1. Restate in his own words what others have said.
2. Sponsor other members.
3. Give encouragement and approval.
4. Formulate and cite examples.
5. Ask questions.

Two matters have been postponed, which will be dealt with now. One concerns group evaluation, and the other deals with preparation.

In diagnosing deficiencies and difficulties in the group operation, the member should assess what is going on by asking himself three questions.

1. Are we following the Group Cognitive Map?
2. Are there any missing Group Roles?
3. Are any of the criteria not being met?

The answers to these three questions should pinpoint the trouble that the group is experiencing—and the remedy.

On the basis of our experience, and that of our colleagues, we present a list of skills that members should acquire to facilitate discussion.

SKILLS USEFUL FOR CLASSROOM DISCUSSION

Before the Discussion

Preparation

a. Start your preparation with a copy of the discussion outline before you.

b. As you read, jot down ideas wherever you think they fit best into the discussion.

c. Look up and learn to say the meanings of new words and concepts.

d. When you have finished reading, go back through the outline and write down reminders of what you might say during each step in the discussion.

e. Practice saying or formulate questions about material you introduce into the discussion.

During the Discussion

Step 1 — Definition of terms and concepts

a. List the words or concepts with which you had some difficulty and ask others to add to your list.

b. Try to define or explain one of the words on your list.

    c.   Ask the group members if you have defined it as they understand it.

    d.   Encourage others to practice explaining what it means to them.

    e.   Restate what someone else has said to make sure you understand it.

    f.   Give an example to clarify the meaning.

    g.   Ask someone else in the group to give an example.

    h.   Ask the group members if everyone understands the new words or concepts.

Step 2 — Statement of the author's message

    a.   State in your own words what you think the assignment was all about.

    b.   Frame a question that will encourage someone else to state what the assignment was about.

    c.   Encourage other group members to practice.explaining it.

    d.   Add to what someone else has said.

    e.   State the ways in which your understanding or interpretation differs from that stated by another member.

    f.   Ask for clarification on points you don't understand.

    g.   Restate what someone else has said if you need to, to be sure you know it.

    h.   If you think two other members are misunderstanding each other, try to lessen the confusion.

Step 3 — Identification of major themes

    a.   Note organization of author's material in terms of headings and subheadings used.

    b.   Consider what makes for a logical sequence of subtopics.

    c.   Write on blackboard, so that all can see the suggested subtopics. This speeds the process and reduces confusion regarding what subtopics are proposed.

Step 4 — Allocation of time

a.   Consider which topics are the most and least difficult to comprehend.

b.   For each subtopic, formulate a question that would initiate a profitable discussion.

c.   Calculate total time remaining and subtract estimated time allocated to steps 6, 7, 8, and 9. This gives time remaining to be distributed among the subtopics.

d.   Do time allocation on blackboard so that all may see what they are agreeing to.

e.   Appoint a timekeeper. Instruct him to announce when the group has two minutes remaining for discussion of a section.

Step 5 — Discussion of major themes and subtopics

a.   Ask the group to state the essential elements of the author's presentation, e.g.:

1.   Hypotheses
2.   Methods
3.   Devices
4.   Techniques
5.   Arguments
6.   Sources

b.   Practice saying for yourself what the author was mainly concerned with and encourage others to do so.

Step 6 — Integration of material with other knowledge

a.   State the meaning or usefulness of the new material in understanding other ideas or concepts.

b.   Phrase questions to put to the group members which will stimulate them to see how the new material fits into what they have studied previously.

c.   Ask or state how the new material contradicts, substantiates, or amplifies some previously developed point.

d.   Summarize into compact statements points others have made.

e.   Listen critically for and try to state puzzling aspects of the material that are giving the group trouble.

f.   Ask for or give help in stating the material more concisely.

g.   Ask another member to restate what he has said if you think you may have misunderstood.

h.   Call the group's attention to and reinforce a comment that seems particularly helpful.

Step 7 — Application of the material

a.   Ask or state why and how the new material can be useful to members.

b.   Give examples of how you might apply it or how the knowledge of it may be useful to you.

c.   Compare to your own experience the author's reasons for thinking it worthwhile.

d.   Test the usefulness of the new material by constructing a situation for which it should be useful.

e.   Give examples you know of which the new material helps to explain or helps you to understand.

Step 8 — Evaluation of author's presentation

a.   State questions to help the group evaluate the new material, the method of arriving at the conclusions, etc.

b.   State points supporting or questioning the validity of the arguments or the reasoning of the author.

c.   State why and how you think the new material is or is not useful.

d.   Frame questions which will help the group to test the usefulness of specific points.

In preparing for a discussion, as in all studying, the student should read the assignment over once to get the general sense of it. For the *LTD* method, he should then approach the article as if he were conducting a silent or fantasy group meeting and prepare contributions that he might make at each step of the cognitive map. A preparation outline is provided, and the kinds of information to be noted are indicated for each step.

OUTLINE FOR PREPARATION

Step One — List all the words of which you are unsure. Look them up and write down the definitions of them.

Step Two — Write down your version of a general statement of the author's message.

Step Three — Identify the subtopics in the article.

Step Four — Note the subtopics which you had trouble comprehending or which you think would provide a profitable discussion.

Step Five — Write out a brief statement of the subject matter of each subtopic. Design a question that you would ask for each.

Step Six — Write down the meaning or usefulness the material has for understanding other concepts. Indicate what other ideas the material substantiates, contradicts, or amplifies.

Step Seven — Write down how the material can apply to your own life situation—past, present or future, or what implications the article has for your own intellectual interests or pursuits.

Step Eight — Write down your reactions and evaluation
of the assignment.

If the student complies with the above preparation outline,
he has learned a great deal before the discussion begins. As
the discussion goes along, he might include additional ideas he
has garnered. The outline then becomes an excellent source of
review for examinations.

If everyone prepares in accordance with the outline above,
the discussion can move along with remarkable ease and
efficiency. When the designated leader inquiries, for example,
what the author's message is, the members need not go into
shock, or start frantically looking through the article, or even
busy themselves trying to think up an answer. All they need
do is share with the group what they have recorded on their
preparation sheets before them. And so it goes for all the
steps of the Group Cognitive Map.

In our experience, we have found it particularly effective
to have the preparation sheets handed in at the end of each
class session. The instructor evaluates them and makes suitable
marginal notes before returning them at the next session. This
feedback enables the student to improve on his preparation
and communicates to him that the instructor takes the preparation sheets seriously. In courses where grades are required,
part of the grade is based on the preparation sheets, as well as
on class participation and examination performance.

EVALUATION

OVER THE LAST TEN years, LTD has been employed by a considerable number of instructors throughout the country. It has been used extensively in the training of probation officers in twenty-five counties in California, as well as in Nevada, Alaska, and Jamaica. It has also been used with school counselors at Idaho State University and the University of Illinois, teaching statistics at the University of Southern California, and sociology at the University of California at Los Angeles, a course in nuclear physics at New York State University at Stony Brook, and with social workers, psychiatric nurses, and clinical psychologists learning group psychotherapy at Brigham Young University, and in educational psychology courses at Snow College, University of Utah, and at the University of Minnesota, to mention a few of the applications and adoptions of LTD. The evaluation by instructors and participants has been uniformly good, with reports either of satisfactory or very satisfactory. The widespread use and the testimonials are offered as evidence of LTD's utility, but they are nonetheless difficult to evaluate quantitatively, and certainly do not represent conclusive evidence.

The significant thing about LTD, or for that matter, any group discussion technique which is properly managed, is that it invariably contributes to the personal development of the individual and also results in his increased involvement in the educational process. We have been urged by our colleagues to expand on these plus values and we are reminded of the many times that a student has been 'turned on' to learning—and we are all painfully aware of the vast numbers who have been 'turned off' by traditional teaching methods. However, we have resisted documenting this aspect of LTD and have concentrated on demonstrating its potential for achieving and enhancing the primary goal of learning course material.

In this regard, one major effort was made at Idaho State University, in which the author taught one section of introductory psychology using the LTD method and his colleague, Dr. Shanna McGee, lectured to the other section. In the second semester, the class was offered again and this time the roles of the instructors were reversed. Each of the classes had between fifty and sixty members. The same multiple-choice, objective type of questions were asked in each section. The results on the examinations were consistent with the findings in other studies of lecture versus discussion, namely, that there was no significant difference in the marks obtained by either method. The trend analysis is worth reporting, however. On the first midterm, the average mark obtained by the lecture method with either instructor was higher than that obtained in the discussion sections. On the second midterm, they were essentially equivalent, whereas on the final there was a noticeable, but not statistically significant, superiority in favor of the discussion sections. When it is remembered that class time was consumed at the beginning of the lecture sessions in learning the method, it is reasonable to entertain the notion that the trend might well be projected to a point where it becomes statistically significant.

The problem of properly evaluating discussion groups is complex, and our attempts to date are admittedly naive. If the claims for discussion groups have any validity, the differences should show up more clearly in follow-up types of evaluations than in achievement on final examinations. Since much time is lost in training students in the method, discussion groups are not properly equated with lecture groups. A more valid comparison would be achieved by using group members who have had previous experience with *LTD*. Also, B. Bloom provides evidence ('The Thought Process of Students in Discussion,' in *Accent on Teaching*, edited by Sidney J. French, New York, Harper, 1954) that somewhat different thought processes prevail in a discussion group than in a lecture. It has been found that significantly more time in a lecture is spent in thinking about and committing facts to memory, whereas in a discussion group, students significantly more often attempt to manipulate ideas. If this is true, we might expect different kinds of exams to produce different results. We might expect objective exams to favor the lecture and easay exams to favor the discussion group. These and other factors will be considered in future research on the process of learning as it occurs in the discussion group. One further comment on the value of LTD. It has been found that when members have been exposed to the method, their performance in seminars and committees has been upgraded and former class members have often reported that they have become more effective members in other group situations. Even more important is the fact that it is possible to teach others to use the method and the materials after having been exposed to the method. In our training of probation officers in group counseling (reported in the *American Behavioral Scientist*, September-October, 1967) more than thirty of the trainees became instructors and proceeded to train other officers in their agency in group counseling. It is important to note that where good instructional material is available, a very good learning situation can occur even though the instructor is not a subject matter expert, if he employs LTD properly. Also, it is worth noting that the problem of large classes with impersonal instruction can be ameliorated by organizing the class into small discussion groups that are instructed in the LTD method.

An important research study on the LTD was conducted by W. D. Gutzmer at the University of Utah in 1969 and is reported as an unpublished doctoral dissertation entitled "A Study in Structured Discussion." Fifteen enrollees in a graduate education course were evaluated on our PMRs and the class meetings were rated on a modified form of the HIM-G. The HIM-G rating scale is derived from the Hill Interaction Matrix (Sage Publications, Beverly Hills, 1970)—a matrix composed of two sets of interacting categories, Content and Work. Results indicated that the early meetings were 'all-over' the matrix but the final session was exclusively in Topic discussion at the two Work levels, Confrontive and Speculative. Also the PMR ratings were uniformly high at the end for all aspects tested. The students were unanimous in rating the LTD highly: eleven of the fifteen said "it was the most useful guide for learning they had ever used in a classroom" and twelve members said they will "use the procedure in their teaching and administration."

It is perhaps instructive to think of LTD as a technological tool similar to programmed instruction and teaching machines. Personally, we do not feel threatened by these devices, but do feel that programmed instruction and teaching machines very effectively impart to an individual, facts and rote memory learnings of impersonal matter. The relevance and personal significance of these learnings are best explored through group discussion. Thus, the innovations in individual teaching are seen as complementary to the LTD method, and the amalgam of all these approaches may well herald a new and exciting era for education.

APPENDIX

POSTMEETING REACTION SHEET

(PMRS)

I. REACTIONS TO GROUP MEETING

Name:_____

Date:_____

Instructions: Mark an X on the line above your response to the following questions.

1. I felt that the group meeting today was:

Excellent   Good   Average   Not So Good   Bad

2. I felt that my participation in the group was:

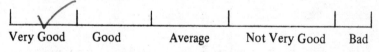

Very Good   Good   Average   Not Very Good   Bad

3. My feelings during the meeting were mainly:

Very   Pleasant   So-So   Unpleasant   Quite
Enjoyable   Unpleasant

4. I felt that I learned from the discussion:

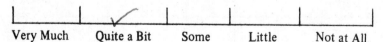

Very Much   Quite a Bit   Some   Little   Not at All

Remarks:

II. EXECUTION OF COGNITIVE MAP

Instructions: For each of the eight steps of the Cognitive Map, indicate your rating of how the group performed the step by placing a check mark in one of the five boxes.

RATINGS

Steps in the Cognitive Map	1 Very Good	2 Quite Adequate	3 Fairly Good	4 Not So Good	5 Poorly
1. Definition of Terms		✓			
2. General Statement			✓		
3. Subtopics Designation			✓		
4. Time Allocation				✓	
5. Subtopic Discussion			✓		
6. Integration		✓			
7. Application		✓			
8. Evaluation			✓		

III. MEMBER ROLES INVENTORY

Instructions: Please check which of the following roles you played some of the time today by making check marks in the A column opposite the roles you played.

Please check which of the following roles you felt were exercised adequately by the group today by making check marks in the B column opposite those roles which were played.

Positive Roles

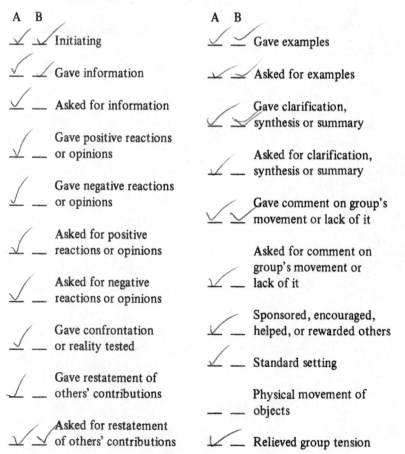

A B
✓ ✓ Initiating

✓ __ Gave information

✓ __ Asked for information

✓ __ Gave positive reactions or opinions

✓ __ Gave negative reactions or opinions

✓ __ Asked for positive reactions or opinions

✓ __ Asked for negative reactions or opinions

✓ __ Gave confrontation or reality tested

✓ __ Gave restatement of others' contributions

✓ ✓ Asked for restatement of others' contributions

A B
✓ ✓ Gave examples

✓ ✓ Asked for examples

✓ ✓ Gave clarification, synthesis or summary

✓ __ Asked for clarification, synthesis or summary

✓ ✓ Gave comment on group's movement or lack of it

✓ __ Asked for comment on group's movement or lack of it

✓ __ Sponsored, encouraged, helped, or rewarded others

✓ __ Standard setting

__ __ Physical movement of objects

✓ __ Relieved group tension

Negative Roles

A B

Acted with aggressiveness
___ ___ and hostility

___ ___ Made self-confessions

Acted with
___ ___ defensiveness

✓ ___ Was competitive

✓ ___ Withdrew

A B

___ ___ Sought sympathy

Pleaded for a pet
___ ___ idea

___ ✓ Horsed around

✓ ___ Was dominating

___ ___ Did some status seeking